I0440920

# Strut in Signature Style: Reinvent Your Wardrobe

Written by Andrea Ward

Published by Consetta Publishing
Copyright© 2008 Essentials by Andi Kamel, LLC
ISBN 978-1438234892
July 2008

# Dedication

This book is dedicated to my loving husband and best friend
Russell T. Ward, for all his support in my career
over the years! Also, in memory of my mother,
Lenore Pauline Glasner Kaplan, who was an inspiration
and visionary in my fashion career. Mom kept me focused with this
special gift in using it to help others.
With much appreciation to my father, Jerry Kaplan and to my sister,
Eileen Chubat, for their creative efforts.

My true passion is motivating women to feel wonderful about
themselves inside and out!

# Strut in Signature Style

## By Andrea Ward

Every woman dreams of taking a limousine to New York City or Europe to the finest shops in the world, and indulging herself in lavish haute couture designs. Even a woman able to shop at that level needs professional guidance in making the right wardrobe choices to create her own individual style.

My background of 35 years in the fashion industry enables me to speak in depth about how to love your clothes with strong inspiration and make great decisions about what you wear. We all know that first impressions count! Your clothes determine how you portray yourself and how others perceive you.

The garment district has offered me the ultimate experience working in the world of artistry on Seventh Avenue. I have learned from many famous fashion houses and publications that forecast all aspects of design. I started as a showroom model for a couture evening wear company striving for a position as a stylist. It was a glamorous life of traveling to all the top specialty stores in the country for exclusive trunk showings, and premiering each season's collections exclusively to the most high profile women in the country.

As I progressed in the business I was asked to dress the actors on the daytime soap operas, assisting on each set, including costumes for gala events. My knowledge comes from the heart and soul of "Fashion Avenue." I am a true "garmento," in the slang we call ourselves. My passion as a long-time retailer and entrepreneur and an innovator of new specialty stores evolved into my becoming a personal wardrobe stylist. I love sharing my knowledge with women and advising them on developing a strong self image that offers them confidence in their personal and professional lives. My quest is that every woman should own a signature wardrobe at any price level.

There are three steps that must take place before assembling your signature wardrobe.  They are:

- Personal assessment
- Evaluation of silhouette, hair and complexion
- Identification of your persona

## Personal Assessment

Personal assessment is the first and utmost step in evaluating your personal and professional lifestyle, and developing an awareness of how you function on a daily basis. Do you travel by plane or car?  What is your profession?  Do you have a young family? Does your day take you directly from work to dining out?  How do you appear from morning to night with the proper attire and a fresh new look? Is your social calendar full?  Are you active, athletic, creative, or busy?  The answers to these questions play a crucial role in your clothing choices.

## Evaluation of Silhouette, Hair and Complexion

The next step is an assessment of your silhouette and body frame, and complexion and hair color. Your physical being and personality type also depicts the image and initiates the route for your personal assessment.  An in-depth look at all of these important components will help you to conceive and understand your persona and will be the foundation of developing a defined style.

# Identification of Your Persona

The third step is identifying your persona. In the world of theatre and fashion when models or actors are trying to market themselves they work on finding this persona. For many it take years, but once you achieve this goal your individuality is resilient inside and out. It is a challenge for most women to see their true selves. Unfortunately many of us are influenced by the media or outside sources that try to dictate how we should look. Elegance, refinement and style can be achieved by anyone in any size, shape or form. Once your persona is acquired you will experience a revitalization of self fulfillment and individuality celebrating your "Independence Day." Bravo to you! Beauty from within will persevere.

This information is pertinent in building the base to your signature wardrobe. Once the information is compiled you can proceed to the next step.

# Looking at What You Own

Next you will view your wardrobe and decide which pieces are the "must haves" and "must not haves." Everyone has favorites they tend to wear more than others, but wouldn't it be great if you could open your closet and just know what works for you. You should own what you actually will utilize in every way, then when you stand back and observe, your closet is merchandised for your every need.

When engaging the services of a wardrobe stylist, trust and respect makes the concept successful, and it is all about relationships. During this process I spend a substantial amount of time with you and in the most intimate spot in your home--your closet, which is usually situated in your bedroom! In addition, I will advise you to discard clothing you have had for years, which you may not want to part with for many reasons. However, the end result is a celebration, based on getting rid of clothing that had no rhyme or reason.  You will feel a renaissance and rebirth.  The observation and analysis is complete!  After this process, you are ready to build your wardrobe, beginning with eight basic pieces.

## The 8 Wardrobe Basics

Every shopping list for proper women's attire should have at least eight basic pieces, which will vary depending on her lifestyle. This example will be directed at the professional woman executive. One of the most important factors in picking these fundamental pieces is the fabric used in the garments. A flat woven fabric cements your wardrobe together.

Imagine a painter beginning an application of paint on a transparent surface, which evolves into layers of shading and becomes more opaque. The final color is resilient and the texture radiates into a magnificent art form. The same philosophy applies to establishing a wardrobe. Begin with an immaculate silhouette, subtle but defined in black, chocolate, midnight, merlot or loden, shades from the riches of the earth. These shades arrived about 10 years ago when a famous fashion designer pioneered the "new black."  Every one of these shades has a black undertone cultivating the way to a vast market of professional women who previously always wore black at a comfort level for work wear. This modern innovation has allowed all designers to create black in every variation, i.e., chocolate brown, midnight navy, loden, merlot, mushroom taupe, and charcoal gray.  Now not only is there a new palette of black, but accessorizing with black meshes with this cutting edge phenomenon.

# Basic #1 and #2

**Black will always be the ultimate choice in classic sophistication.** Your first choice and purchase should be a clean and timeless black suit. In theory, once you have made that initial investment the next choice should be a chocolate or midnight suit. In terms of practicality your black suit should be a three-piece ensemble consisting of jacket, pant and skirt. If the suit has only a pant or skirt, the second shade should be able to interact with the black suit. My preference would be chocolate, as it is lush against black and will offer many options.

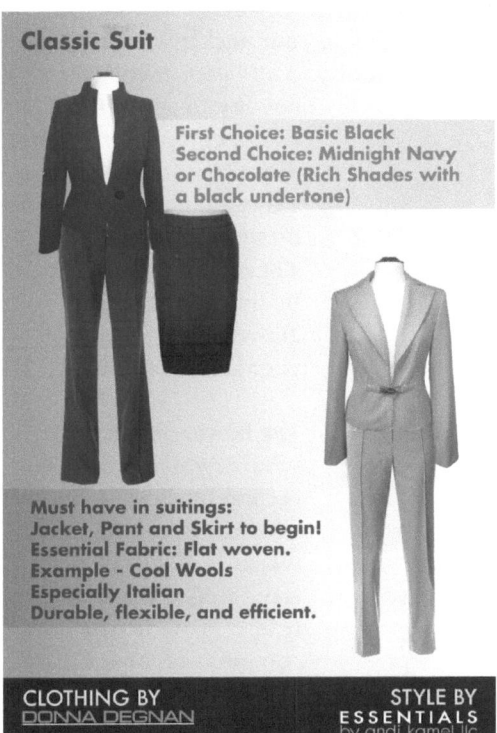

**Classic Suit**

First Choice: Basic Black
Second Choice: Midnight Navy
or Chocolate (Rich Shades with
a black undertone)

Must have in suitings:
Jacket, Pant and Skirt to begin!
Essential Fabric: Flat woven.
Example - Cool Wools
Especially Italian
Durable, flexible, and efficient.

CLOTHING BY
DONNA DEGNAN

STYLE BY
ESSENTIALS
by andi kamel llc

## Basic #3

The third basic is a basic dress, preferably black, made from woven fabric. The neckline of the dress should be a jewel or square neck it should sit perfectly under a jacket and frame your neck and face softly. The dress neckline gives you the opportunity to add your favorite

Classic Dress

Always in basic **Black**

Must Have!
Teamed up with classic jacket
Variation in sleeve lengths

CLOTHING BY
DONNA DEGNAN

STYLE BY
ESSENTIALS
by andi kamel llc

jewelry to adorn the whole composition. The dress should have either a three-quarter sleeve or be sleeveless. If it is long sleeved, the fabric should be thin and smooth, allowing you to slide your jacket over it.

The fabric can be cool wool or you can seek out techno fabrics. Techno is a high-tech textile that works in any season and is durable and wrinkle free. It is made of a combination of viscose rayon and polyester. Even the most famous fashion designers use this modern technology, resulting in the most refined fabrics that exist today in the high end market. Couture collections depict sport pieces made in techno fabric. It usually has some stretch that gives your fit comfort and ease, feels supple and looks sleek. Techno can be mixed with cool wools, depending on the silhouette and style.

Remember, it can be worn 12 months out of the year, is travel-friendly and machine washable. Cool wools have a 9-month wearability and usually are wrinkle free. They should be dry cleaned only.

8

## Basic #4

The next basic is a pant or trouser.  It is important that this piece stand on its own and represent a classic style with a touch of trendiness. It can be a clean silhouette with new pocket treatment. The choice should be a favorite fit and a designer or resource that you feel terrific in. This is an item that will coordinate with your suit jackets or novelty jackets demonstrating a more casual, but pulled together image. Charcoal gray or soft gray would be a great way to offer a softer personality to the basic choices you have made.

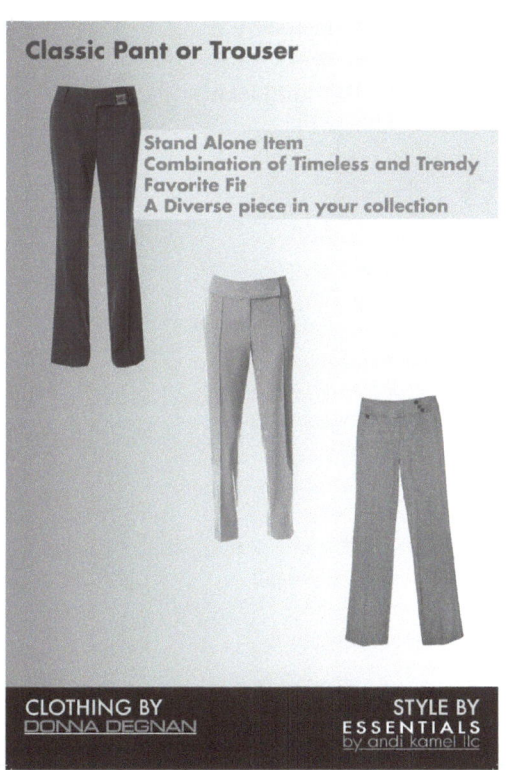

**Classic Pant or Trouser**

Stand Alone Item
Combination of Timeless and Trendy
Favorite Fit
A Diverse piece in your collection

CLOTHING BY
DONNA DEGNAN

STYLE BY
ESSENTIALS
by andi kamel llc

9

## Basic #5

The basic skirt is sassy and with a slight attitude in style, but still in the timeless category. This piece should work independently for variety in daytime to dinner dressing. The skirt should also be able to work with at least one of the suit jackets to tell a new story.

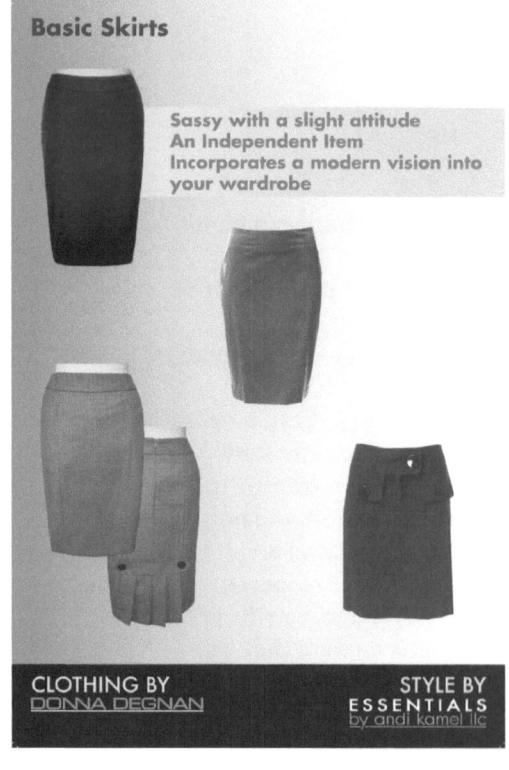

**Basic Skirts**

Sassy with a slight attitude
An Independent Item
Incorporates a modern vision into your wardrobe

CLOTHING BY
DONNA DEGNAN

STYLE BY
ESSENTIALS
by andi kamel llc

## Basic #6

Basic #6 should be a colorful jacket, still maintaining the same fabric choice (woven or cool wool). Depending on the shades that were chosen in suitings and the other basics, a pastel in pale blue or a classic neutral such as camel hair would certainly incorporate into this palette.

# Basic #7

This basic is a novelty jacket. It may be done as soft dressing in a silhouette that can be worn over all of your basic choices. Black, chocolate, soft gray and camel hair are all good color choices, in a herringbone or a fabric that has slight texture. It should integrate with all of your basic choices in both color and style. This jacket will give a contrast of two-toned definition within a monotone effect, adding depth to your flat woven fabrics and giving an element of surprise to all of your basic choices. This is crucial for layering--it will make a statement and tie your wardrobe together.

NOVELTY ITEMS

Fashion pieces that add the *edge*

and *drama* to your wardrobe

CLOTHING BY
DONNA DEGNAN

STYLE BY
ESSENTIALS
by andi kamel llc

*"My designs are classic, but I keep in mind the woman who wants fashion forward clothing, so you will find my designs to be interestingly fashionable, yet timeless."*
*- Hilton Hollis*

## Basic #8

The crisp white shirt has become a must-have in the basic wardrobe and enlightens your clothing and glistens against a women's skin.  A charming well known French designer is noted for her beautiful white shirts. Romance and femininity make the white shirt one of the most significant items in recent time that has upstaged any other top in the market today. It is seen on celebrities, news anchors and business women and is always fresh and tasteful.  The price range of the white shirt varies but is always made of cotton, with or without stretch. The detail and treatment varies from puckers to ruffles and different collar shapes. When purchasing a shirt it must fit the formula and balance of design and be a style that will join your collection appropriately.

**Underpinnings**

Shells, Tees - Layering pieces
Multi Fabric choices: Cotton, silk, techno fabrics

Always plays a starring role in your Ensemble!

CLOTHING BY
DONNA DEGNAN

STYLE BY
ESSENTIALS
by andi kamel llc

## Basic #8A

The *underpinning* is defined as a shell or tee-shirt. The underpinning is a very important part of your ensemble and is noticed first since it is at eye level whether you are sitting or standing. The integrity of your clothes comes from the coordination of your underpinning.  In addition, it says a lot about you. This semi-basic in essence is in two categories.  It debuts in the basics but it takes on a new position as a component basic which I will discuss later. Keep in mind that your underpinning is always the star and the wovens play supporting roles.

Underpinning fabrics should be silk, cashmere, merino wool, cotton, or techno fabrics. It is important that the fabric is comfortable against your skin.

The tee-shirt is an item that needs to be addressed now as a fashion icon. Who would have thought that the top international fashion houses would be selling this piece of clothing at $300, or for that matter $100? It certainly is a gem and is worn by everyone whether it is down-and-dirty casual or with the most upscale suit. It is has made history repeatedly and always comes out smelling like a rose. This funny little flimsy fabric that looks like underwear as we remember it has maintained American heritage and has traveled and evolved to the runways of Europe's finest fashion houses. It is the number one fun favorite to wear anytime and anywhere. Tees can be made of cotton, silk, wool, cashmere and all of the techno fabrics such as supplex, polyamid, tencel, microfiber and many others.

## Summary of the 8 Basics:

- Suit with pant
- Suit with skirt (varying shade of black with black undertone)
- Black dress
- Pant or trouser
- Skirt
- Colored jacket
- Tweed jacket
- White shirt
- Underpinning

## Component Basics

As I mentioned earlier, the category known as component basics are a subdivision of the basics and help to give your wardrobe density.  They are:

- Underpinning in different fabric
- Pant in different fabric
- Skirt in different fabric
- Classic pieces branching out with more variety in fabric and style.

*"Style and fashion will change but one thing remains constant...women want to feel and look pretty. When it comes to fashion, every woman has to find her own unique look and style and be true to it. This style is your image to the world and should reflect who you are inside and not necessarily what is in Vogue".*
*- Donna Degnan*

## Underpinnings in More Depth

An underpinning can also be called shell, blouse, tee, or knit top.  As I mentioned earlier, underpinnings will always be the stars.  They are the pieces that pop your suit or any ensemble, and should be made from an array of different fabrics and knit blends, such as cotton, silk, cashmere and soft merino wools.  They can also be in techno fabrics that include supplex, inspiring comfort and ease. Tencel, made from the bark of a tree (cellulose) is soft and supple.  Even microfiber plays a role in combination with these fabrics.

The variety of style is endless and certainly depends on what you are wearing.  The classic silhouette often is defined as a tee in a jewel neck, square neck, bateau, v-neck, scoop, or turtleneck.  This is where you have to assess what you own and the balance of style, as well as the weight of the fabrics.  For example, a woven suit with a chunky angora sweater is a "fashion don't."

In conclusion, with underpinnings, keep in mind there are an extensive styles, fabrics and colors to choose from.  Caution is the word.

Important considerations when choosing underpinnings are:

- Shape
- Style
- Fabric or knit type
- Neckline
- Shade or color
- Solid, texture or print
- Care and efficiency

All of the above will help you when shopping for layering pieces. Think about how you will coordinate new pieces with what you already own.

## Classic Fashion

### Novelty Items

These pieces bring novelty and excitement to your wardrobe.  They are the drama and pizzazz that frost the signature aspect to your clothing. This part of the concept has to be done with grace and charm. But at the same time it is fun and inspirational to look at what's hot and what's not and ask if it would it work in your wardrobe.  It is like learning a new step in a dance and must be in sync or it will clash.

*Clothing design by Hilton Hollis*
*Photo Copyright by John Novajosky*

## Accessorizing

- **Shoes**
- **Handbags**
- **Belts**
- **Hosiery**
- **Scarves**
- **Jewelry and Artwear**

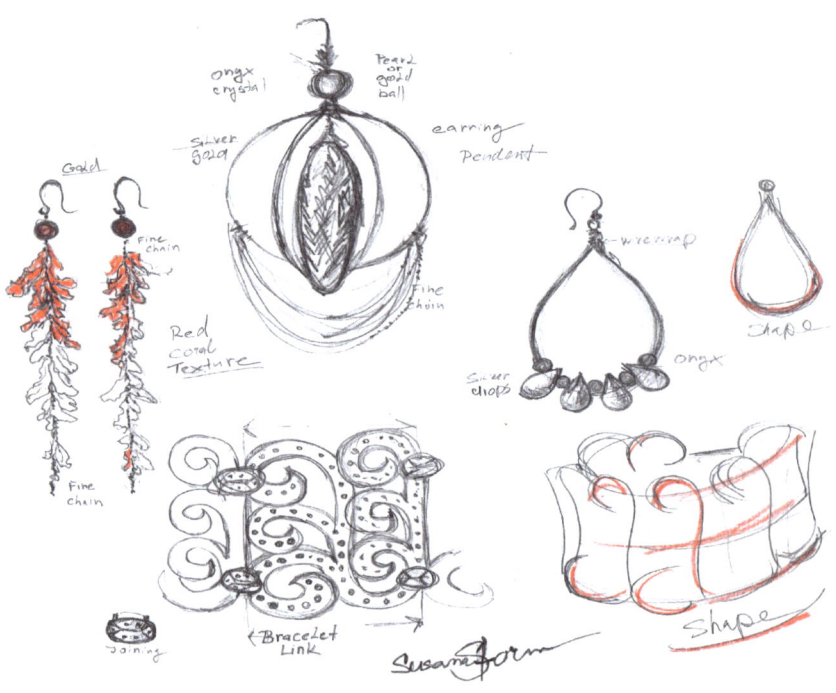

Accessories add to the drama of your wardrobe. They are the last details that represent the artistry of dressing. Done improperly, they can turn a beautiful tailored piece into a fashion faux pas. Accessories contribute to the portrayal of your overall image that you have been challenged to develop articulately in your personal assessment. They depict your personal style and should maintain the theme of your clothing collection.

Bags, shoes and belts should be made of leather or suede. Scarves should be from silk, cotton, wool or techno fabrics. Don't forget jewelry in silver or gold, including gemstones.

## A Style Week at a Glance

*Clothing design by Hilton Hollis*
*Photo Copyright by John Novajosky*

The complexity of choosing appropriate pieces for your wardrobe can be overwhelming, but if you follow this strategy and break it down, it will be much easier. Looking back at the steps to get to this point should make it very natural for you to now make great choices. You have delved deep down and have gotten to know your true inner core. All of this has paved the way to creating your own signature wardrobe.

## Monday

Your work week begins on Monday morning as you arrive at the office sporting a classic blazer in a multi-black and ivory tweed. This novelty jacket is teamed up with a black slim flat woven pant from the basics. Popped with the crisp white cotton shirt (underpinning), it makes a fresh and clean choice for the first day of the week. A business lunch is scheduled at your local bistro to meet a potential client. It is someone from the art world, so you drape a stark patterned scarf with accents of lemon and rouge to captivate a subtle glow to your complexion. As you are seated your guest's first impression is the artistry in your choice of art deco design with the tweed geometric pattern, each piece maintaining its own clarity. Your afternoon appointments are loyal clients and follow-up business so you slip your jacket off and the crisp white shirt adorned by the scarf depicts an elegant dressed-down look.

## Tuesday

Tuesday you have an early formal business appointment. Your day will be long and rigorous but your image has to be impeccable. The finale of this day is an important dinner meeting with an upscale company's CEOs. Your choice is your black dress sculpted for your figure in double face wool, making a clean silhouette. It has soft lines, a jewel neckline and three-quarter sleeves, showing quiet elegance. The dress is a timeless knee length and worn with hose in true nude so sheer they are transparent.

Footwear is a simple black pump in fabric or the softest leather. In creating the ultimate ensemble, a Chanel style novelty jacket in cerulean blue offers a splash of color. Finished off with a neckpiece in sterling, onyx and pearl, you look breezy and cool. A flat black bag with a thin shoulder strap softly floats over your shoulder and your matching black portfolio sits under your arm, gracefully emanating your persona. The versatility of this clothing comes through as evening approaches and you remove your jacket for dinner and replace it with a black cashmere wrap you have discreetly stashed in your portfolio. You arrive looking fabulous!

## Wednesday

By midweek you are in full swing with appointments, and a staff meeting to end the day. For morning appointments out of the office you appear in your staple--a black suit in a classic design but with a modern edge. The fabric choice is efficient for travel and always appears fresh. Sleek and tailored, this piece is acceptable anywhere in your itinerary from daytime to dinner and should always consist of three pieces—jacket, pant and skirt. If you are traveling you may choose the pant for mobility and flexibility, depending on the weather. The black silhouette with a smooth silk blouse in ivory with your favorite pearls will glisten as you run through your busy morning. It is late afternoon and you are back in the office ready to discuss important matters with the staff. You want to look professional and project calmness so you slip off your jacket. Your blouse and pearls are what everyone is viewing as you discuss matters at hand. Remember, your underpinning always plays the starring role in any ensemble.

## Thursday

As you start to wind down your work week there is still a day of meetings on premise and the clients you will see today are familiar loyal business associates. You enter the board room to meet your first appointment with a racy cashmere cardigan set in silver gray at finger tip length representing the soft jacket image. You are playing the monotone heather tones with a classic charcoal gray pant. A black pressed leather belt offers texture and new dimension to this soft creamy look. The matte silver buckle inspires the sheer artistry becoming the focal point at your waist. As a last minute dinner date arises at a restaurant that calls for more formal attire, you fortunately have brought along your black suit jacket. You escape with jacket in hand looking as appropriate for the occasion as if it had been planned.

## Friday

Ahh!! The end of the work week is here and you will still be seeing a few clients today. To celebrate a successful week of business accomplishments you are meeting a group of friends at a trendy restaurant in town after your business day is over. You arrive in the classic black skirt suit and surplice top in soft pink mohair. It makes a great underpinning but is a little racy for day. Keep it classic for daytime by wearing the jacket, but when ready to go out to dinner, slip your jacket off and add a pair of fun black boots. You may add a wrap in a pattern over the soft pink top or an interesting accessory piece at the neck or ears.

A great working wardrobe must function with flexibility, efficiency and durability.  Your clothes should work for you and the last detail is to debut with a total look for the modern woman. The signature wardrobe will offer inspiration in your life and bring a new-found awareness that brings confidence in any setting.

## How to Merchandise Your Closet

- Organize pieces by color
- Organize pieces from light to dark
- Organize pieces by weight of fabric
- Organize pieces from short to long
- Suits should hang together
- Separates should hang together
- Basics and component basics should be arranged for easy access

All of your clothing should be hanging and placed in strategic arrangement. This will give you efficient access to your pieces on a daily basis. Organization is important if you have made this investment to own a signature wardrobe. The aura of your closet should represent this immaculate image.

I hope I have enlightened you on wardrobe techniques and the world of fashion. As in any industry, there are many facets to understand. Most importantly, the message I want to convey is to develop your own style; it is crucial. The choices you make regarding your clothing purchases, regardless of budget should always be carefully thought through.

Most of the time when we make a spontaneous purchase, we say, "I don't know why I bought this. I never wear it!" Or the famous words, "I am going out and I have nothing to wear!" Tons of clothes in the closet! Bad choices! In the end it should be fun. And you should feel terrific in what you are wearing!

*Remember, Strut in Signature Style!*

## About the Author

Andrea Ward, author of *Strut in Signature Style - Reinvent Your Wardrobe*, has 35 years of experience working in the garment industry as a merchant, manufacturer, model, stylist and consultant. She is called upon by many as a personal stylist for professional women.

Andrea's career began in New Haven, Connecticut where she was employed by Ann Taylor when it was privately owned by Richard Leibeskind, Founder.

She moved on to New York where she became a stylist for a Fashion Couture House known as Richilene. Her position at Richilene was working as a stylist for Elizabeth Arden Salons and many glamorous specialty stores such as Lilli Rubin, Martha and Sara Fredericks. She would represent the company by featuring private showings for clients and guests in these locations. Some of the celebrities that Andrea has worked with are Jill St. John, Lucky Roosevelt and the Supremes.

The Richilene Collection was well known in social circles and was frequently written up in Town and Country with the young Debutantes and infamous parties such as the Cotton Ball in Memphis and the Kentucky Derby. The opportunity to work in a capacity such as this one was a lifetime experience seeing how the rich and famous lived and dressed. Andrea Ward worked with the finest fabrics and top designers.

Andrea married her husband Russ in 1985 and landed back in Connecticut and started a specialty store called Andrea Renee' Limited, in Southbury which she owned for 2 years.

Her next opportunity was to work with the largest manufacturer in Western Europe known as Steilmann. The goal was to open retail stores in the U.S. with European ready to wear clothing. The company was based in Germany and her position was to develop this multi store operation. She spent 5 years achieving this goal and when she left the company there were 25 stores. She traveled to the German market 8 times a year. Andrea found it to be very exciting to have worked with Karl Lagerfeld's ready to wear collection.

Her passion was to own her own business and so in 1995 she opened Andrea Ward Clothier in New Haven and was in business for 12 years. When she closed she was honored with *"The Small Business Award"* from the Chamber of Commerce. Her concept was built on being very civic minded and philanthropic.

Presently, Andrea Ward is the owner of Essentials by Andi Kamel LLC, which offers the total look in dressing for the modern woman.

**For more on Andrea please visit:**
 www.andreawardrobe.com


**I would love to hear your questions, comments and feedback! You can email me at** andrea@andreawardrobe.com

**- Andrea Ward**

## Special Thanks

To my mentors and supporters, past and present that helped me to navigate through my career and the garment industry:

Angie Rossi – Angie was one of the original supervisors for Ann Taylor when it was privately owned.

Isabel Grogan – Manager of the former store, Esther's.

Ilene and Richard Pacun - Owners of the former Richilene Company which was known for couture evening wear.

Seymour Levy – Ready to Wear Designer

Randy Kemper - Ready to Wear Designer
Meg Agnew of Randy Kemper

Adri – Special friend and Designer.

Nadia Abdella – Designer for Adri

Renee Ripinsky - Special friend and clothing specialist

Yansi Fugel – Designer
Naomi Foreman of Yansi Fugel
Melissa Hayes of Yansi Fugel

Donna Degnan - Designer
Sue Horn of Donna Degnan
Ellen Moore of Donna Degnan

Hilton Hollis - Designer
Jessie Riley of Hilton Hollis

Susana Storm - Designer

Angela Katz of Max Mara, USA
Pranith Gunasena of Max Mara, USA

Linda, owner of J'envie

Annie Kolton – Former owner of Drama
Denise - Special friend

A very special thanks to Bruni Butschek Beckman, an icon in the garment industry and a true mentor and inspiration to myself and my career. She introduced me to the European market and invited me to partner with her to open numerous stores in the states. I was very fortunate to experience working with her.

To my friend and colleague, Lori Quaranta, (www.consettapr.com ) who inspired me to publish this book and share my knowledge with women everywhere!

Front Cover Art reprinted with permission by Donna Degnan
Back Cover Photo and Design reprinted with permission by Hilton Hollis
Jewelry Art and Design reprinted with permission by Susana Storm
Book Cover Design by Vaughan Davidson www.killercovers.com

Published by Consetta Publishing 2008

www.ingramcontent.com/pod-product-compliance
Lightning Source LLC
Chambersburg PA
CBHW050928290526
45792CB00002B/929